Anonymous

Reference Book

Interesting facts and valuable information for packers of fruits, vegetables

and oysters

Anonymous

Reference Book
Interesting facts and valuable information for packers of fruits, vegetables and oysters

ISBN/EAN: 9783337370060

Printed in Europe, USA, Canada, Australia, Japan

Cover: Foto ©Lupo / pixelio.de

More available books at **www.hansebooks.com**

REFERENCE BOOK

(ILLUSTRATED)

INTERESTING FACTS AND VALUABLE
INFORMATION FOR PACKERS
OF

Fruits, Vegetables and Oysters.

THE · WARFIELD · MANUFACTURING · CO.

Nos. 336, 338, 340 and 342 North Street,

BALTIMORE, MD.

Manufacturers of Special Machinery.

COMPLIMENTS OF
S. DAVIES WARFIELD,
President.

GREETING.

THIS BOOK is designed to supply such "points" in connection with the canning of fruits and vegetables as may
be useful to the packer of those articles; together with the
best and latest appliances to produce the *finest grade of goods*
at the *least possible cost.*

The writer, by reason of his association with a company whose
special line of manufacture has been that of machinery for canning
purposes, whose success in the construction of new or patented
appliances for the use of packers is well known to the trade, and
in addition being largely interested, personally, in the packing
of vegetables, etc., and in his own packing houses having had
the advantage of *personally testing* such articles of machinery as
may be herein recommended, feels that the experience gained
from such sources should qualify him, to *some* extent at least,
for the work he has undertaken.

Respectfully,

S. D. WARFIELD,

PRESIDENT, THE WARFIELD MFG. CO.

BALTIMORE, *January*, 1889.

"My Maryland" 's a grand old State,
To give us food "for tin,"—
Not only a "wrapper for the goods,"
But also "what's within."

Our Bay affords us oysters fine,
Our lands, fruits, and vegetables too;
And now to pack them good and cheap,
It gives us "Warfield" this to do.

ONE MOMENT,—

What a luxury, to have on our table in the midst of winter the various fruits and vegetables, retaining all the richness and flavor of their natural state before going into the can !

Each year has marked some improvement in the method of preparing the different varieties of food for canning, until now, with the various appliances and improved machinery at command, the careful packer is enabled to preserve each article in hermetically sealed cans, to be opened months afterwards—yea, even years—as good, rich and nice as when first packed. Thus has the canning industry become one of the greatest of the country, employing thousands of hands, and giving to the world food in convenient packages which may be transported to the most remote corner of the globe.   .

Baltimore has long been recognized as the great center of the canning industry of the country, and it is unquestionably the most important industry of Maryland in operation at present, particularly when considering the immense force of workers it employs, Harford County, Maryland, containing the greatest number of packing-houses of any county in the United States.

The fruit and vegetable packing season begins in May and continues until about October, the various articles being packed in about the following order :

Early June Peas,	Marrowfat Peas,	Tomatoes,
Pineapples,	Raspberries,	Peaches,
Strawberries,	Whortleberries,	Pears,
Gooseberries,	Blackberries,	Lima Beans,
String Beans,	Green Gages,	Corn,
Cherries,	Damsons,	Apples.

The labor employed in the packing trade is composed largely of Bohemians, who are very hard-working people, and if permitted, will work twenty hours out of the twenty-four. They all work—men, women, boys and girls; and there can be no more interesting sight than a visit to a large canning factory when in full operation—the mother, with her entire family—the baby rolled in a blanket, asleep, tucked away on some convenient box, while she, with her boys and girls, are at work to procure the means with which to support their home.

It can be said that there are no "hours of labor" about the packing house in busy season, as they are at work on perishable goods which *must be put up*.

Wages are paid mostly by "piece work," and vary according to the article being packed.

The Oyster season runs from about the middle of October until March.

Nothing is so essential to the successful packing of goods as *good water, plenty of it*, and convenient to the canning factory.

Another important feature is to have sufficient capacity, particularly *steam* capacity, to meet any emergency which may arise in the heart of the busy season; for the canning season is a busy one, and each article of machinery should be in its place, tested and *known to be right* before starting. Then to exercise judgment in the procuring of the *best* goods to put up, observing cleanliness in the various departments of the business, not only in the preparation of the goods for the can, but in the care of the cans after being packed.

Often has the sale of a nice lot of goods been ruined by the bad appearance of the cans or boxes. Therefore it is advisable that goods should be stored in a house that can be *closed up*.

It is highly important to have accurate thermometers and gauges on the process kettles, for upon their accuracy depends, in a large measure, the quality of the goods. They should be tested from time to time to insure their perfection.

In the selection of such machines or machinery as may be necessary to the business, let the *first* consideration be to procure that which will produce the *best quality* of goods; *cheapening* in the preparation of the same by saving of labor, while a very important point of course, should be a *secondary* consideration, for a fine grade of goods will *always* bring its worth, whereas a *cheap* grade *often* sells cheap.

Let the main object of the packer be—*how nice he can make his goods*, not *how many he can pack*—" quality rather than quantity."

SUGAR CORN.

There is no article "in tin," in which the past two or three seasons have marked greater advancement than in sugar corn, not only in quality and "mode of putting up," but in the expeditious and cleanly manner of handling the same.

Isaac Winslow, of Portland, Me., is supposed to have been the first to pack sugar corn in hermetically sealed cans for sale. His first experiments were made in about the year 1842, and in the year 1863 he obtained letters patent of the United States for the invention. He was the uncle of the well-known Jno. Winslow Jones who will be remembered from the celebrated Jones-McMurray suit, when Mr. Jones sued Louis McMurray of Maryland, in 1874, for infringement of the Winslow patents referred to. Mr. Jones lost his suit, and thus the packing of sugar corn became general throughout the country. It may be well to state here that Louis McMurray (lately deceased) operated the largest corn-packing establishment in the world. This factory is located at Frederick, Md., and has a capacity of 150,000 cans per day.

The principal varieties of seed in use are "Stowell's Evergeeen" and "Egyptian," the former being largely the favorite, it being a hardy plant and yielding largely to the acre. In the selection of seed, care should be exercised to procure good, sound seed, northern grown being preferred by many packers.

Planting should begin about May 1st, provided the season is sufficiently advanced, and continued at intervals, according to the acreage to be planted, until about June 20th—sugar corn planted later than this rarely amounting to much. The proper preparation of the land before planting is a very important item ; thoroughly prepared land being equivalent to *one working*. If planted by hand, not less than 4 to 6 grains should be dropped to the hill to insure "a stand," thinning out after the corn comes up to two stalks in the hill. Most growers prefer to use a corn-drill for planting their corn, preferably one that will checker the corn to be worked both ways.

Experience has proven that it pays to use some good fertilizer for sugar corn, sown with a wheat-drill before planting, a little being used in the corn-drill when planting, or dropped on hill if planted by hand.

Sugar corn requires *good* land. The corn should be well worked while young, and every effort made to secure a good "stand" at first planting, replanting rarely turning out much. In pulling the corn it is highly important to have it young and tender ; better be a little too green than too old. It should not be piled too high in the husking yard, 18 inches to 2 feet is high enough, to prevent heating. Corn should never be allowed to lie in the yard longer than possible, it should be worked up promptly in the order that the loads arrive, allowing only the last loads to lie over night to make a start in the morning.

A fair *average* for a crop of corn, *taken all through*, is about 50 to 60 cases per acre, although as high as 150 cases are produced on a single acre. About 2½ tons per acre (weighed in the husk) is a fair average for a crop, taken all through. As high as 6 tons, however, are grown to a single acre. It depends entirely upon the character of the soil and care given the crop. The factories of Maryland open on corn about the middle of August. The corn is husked by the basket, 2 or 3 cents per basket being paid.

After the corn is husked it is ready to be cut from the cob. It is advisable to have the ears "picked over" or "culled" before going to the machines, throwing out bad or defective ears.

It might be well to call attention at this point to the two modes of packing corn, known as the Eastern or "dry pack," and the Maryland or "moist pack." It will be understood that an entirely different process of handling the corn is employed in these two methods.

For the purpose of removing the grain from the cob, the most successful and practical machine on the market is the "*Warfield Patent Cutter.*" This machine (a cut of which is given, together with a few extracts from letters received, on page 28) is strongly built of iron (weight 600 lbs) and can be run by hand or steam power (steam power preferably). It is positively the only practical machine manufactured possessing the advantage of being capable of adjustment to cut the grain *whole* from the cob without *mashing* (according to the Maryland or "moist" style of pack), leaving the grain as whole as when cut by hand ; or the grain can be cut *at any depth desired* and the balance *scraped* from the cob (according to the Eastern or " dry " pack).

Thus it will be seen that the owner of this machine is enabled to pack *either* or *both* of the two styles of pack mentioned above, it simply being a matter of the adjustment of the cutter.

The " Warfield Cutter " has been in use a number of years, during which time it has been steadily improved, all weak points being corrected, and it is now generally regarded as the best and most complete machine for its purpose in existence. There is practically no waste when using the cutter, and the corn cut by the same is of superior quality.

The Maryland or "moist" pack will first be described.

In the first place, the knives of the cutting machines are set to cut the grain *close to the cob*, in close imitation of " hand cutting." So perfectly will this machine (Warfield) perform this operation that it is impossible to tell the difference between corn cut by hand and that cut by the machine. For this grade of corn, one set of "scrapers " (4) is removed from the machine, the other set (4) being set to bear very lightly on the cob, sufficiently hard to press some of the milk therefrom. Thus you get the whole grain with sufficient milk to retain the *natural flavor* of sugar corn.

After the corn is cut from the cob it is poured into the "silking" machine, which separates from the grain the silk and particles of husk and cob that may be therein.

The best machine for this purpose, and the one now in almost general use, is the " *Warfield Silking Machine*," cut of which is given on page 38. It has very large capacity, silking thoroughly 25,000 to 30,000 cans per day, is strongly constructed, and can be readily cleaned while in operation.

From the " Silker " the corn is filled into the cans (2 lb). This is accomplished by means of the *Warfield-Nichols Can Filler*, cut of which is shown on page 41, **The Warfield Manufacturing Company** being sole manufacturers of the same. This machine automatically carries the cans under the filling mechanism, which measures and puts the required amount of corn into each can, then discharges the filled cans at the other end of the machine. It has a filling attachment for putting the requisite quantity of brine in each can, which can be detached if desired, and the cans "dipped " or filled with brine by means of the " Dipping Machine," to be described later on, as many packers prefer to "dip" the cans after being filled with corn. This "Filler" can be adjusted to put any quantity of corn into the can desired; it is run by steam power, and will fill 25 to 35,000 cans per day.

Another method of filling is by means of a metal plate through which a number of holes are cut corresponding to the number of holes in the cans when packed closely together on the packing table. This plate is surrounded by a wooden frame. A sufficient quantity of corn is weighed to fill the cans, poured into the apparatus, and worked into the cans.

The quantity of corn necessary to *properly fill* a can, or to produce a "standard" can of corn, must be regulated by the packer; it varies according to the condition of the corn. It requires more weight of corn to fill when young and tender than when the corn *is older*. A can should "cut out full of corn," and the aim of the packer should be to produce a full can of young and tender corn, well cleaned and of bright color; must not be *too full*, or the can is likely to either burst in the process or "swell" after same.

After being filled with corn, the brine is next put into the can. The *only machine* for this purpose is the "*Warfield-Winters Can Dipping Machine.*"

This machine (shown on page 42) runs by steam power, and is connected to a brine cask by a pipe provided with a valve, thus permitting as much brine to flow into the machine as the cans in filling take therefrom. The cans are placed in one end of the machine, are automatically carried through, *filled, drained,* and discharged at the other end. This machine is a model of perfection in its way, and will fill and drain in the most perfect manner, putting the requisite quantity of brine into each can, from 25 to 30,000 cans per day.

From the "Dipping Machine" the cans are placed in trays, the tops "wiped" (to clean the groove where the cap is soldered) and caps put on. They are then taken to the "*Warfield-Winters Capping Machine,*" where the cans are capped. This machine can be operated by any one of ordinary intelligence, and is strongly and compactly built. Cut of the machine will be found on page 45.

The cans are now ready for the "exhaust." This consists in expelling or "exhausting" the air from the can through the "tip" hole which has been left open when the cans were capped, by immersing them in boiling water.

The old method for "exhausting" was to place the cans in crates holding one layer each. These crates were then lowered by a crane into tubs containing boiling water, where they were allowed to remain the requisite length of time. A number of tubs were necessary to accomplish this result, and great care exercised to take the time each crate of cans was put in the exhaust, in order to give the proper time. The extra handling of the cans from the exhaust to the process crates was also a disadvantage and expense. The "*Warfield-Winters Exhauster*" has supplanted the old method (See cut, page 46.)

This machine is run by steam power, and is so constructed as to be adjusted to give the cans the proper time for exhaust, thereby dispensing with the necessity of "taking the time" when the goods are put in. The same trays in which the cans are placed from the capping machines are put in the "exhauster" at one end, automatically carried through the boiling water-bath and delivered at the other end of the machine to the tipping bench, having received the proper time. The cans are now "tipped" in the same tray in which they came through the machine, the trays are then placed in the "*Warfield Test Tub*" (see cut on page 47), where they are lowered into boiling water to test the cans and caps. This "test tub" is a very simple and convenient contrivance for testing cans and is easily worked. From the "test tub" the cans are placed in the process crates. It will thus be seen that there has been no change of cans from the trays in which they were placed at the capping machines, to the process kettle, dispensing entirely with the exhaust crates, tubs, and crane fixtures for hoisting the exhaust crates; also dispensing with the additional handling of cans necessary with the old method, and the "keeping of time"—the "exhauster" taking the place of the entire " old time " outfit.

For the purpose of "processing" or "cooking" goods "in tin," the "*Shriver Patent Process Kettle*" is the most popular now on the market. This kettle, a cut of which will be found on page 48, is manufactured exclusively by **The Warfield Manufacturing Company**, and possesses the advantage of being adapted for use with either *dry steam* or *steam and water;* the steam and water process being generally considered the *safest and best* principle for cooking goods. By the use of this kettle and its appliances, a uniform heat is obtained, and the large number now in use fully attest its superiority over any other processing apparatus manufactured.

After the crates are taken from the kettle they are lowered into the cooling tub (containing cold water) and allowed to remain until the cooking process going on in the can when taken from the kettle is checked ; afterwards the crates are placed on the floor truck (page 55) and conveyed where desired. Thus is completed, in the most approved manner, the packing of corn by the Maryland or "moist" pack.

Now the Eastern or "dry" pack. For this class of goods, the knives of the cutting machines are set to cut the grain to about one-half its depth, the full complement of "scrapers" (two sets, eight in all) are left on the machine and set to scrape from the cob, the remaining portion of the grain not cut by the knives; thus removing from the cob all the corn—part in the form of grain, the balance in the form of "pulp."

There are two methods of handling the corn cut in this manner : one is by means of the steaming process, as follows :

After passing through the "silking" machine, the corn is poured into the "*Hemingway Cooker or Steamer.*" For "dry packed" or "heavy scraped" corn, this machine is a great success, not only as a labor-saving machine, but for quality of goods.

The "automatic feeder," into which the corn is poured, feeds the corn into the machine, through which it is carried by an "endless screw" or "conveyor," being steamed in transit through the machine. The filling attachment at its end forces the corn into the cans. This "steamer" differs from any machine of its kind on the market in its principle of "steaming"; not only does steam enter the outer casing or "jacket" of the machine, but the "screw" or "conveyor" is hollow, and of such construction as to allow of steam being admitted directly to the corn ; a very important point, and possessed *only by this steamer.*

The cut on page 49 shows the construction and mode of operating this "steamer." **The Warfield Manufacturing Company** are sole agents for sale of these machines. From the steamer the cans, after being wiped, go to the capping machine (page 45), then to the "test tub" (page 47), and to the process kettle (page 48), the "steaming process" taking the place of the "exhaust," the cans are capped and "tipped" at same time.

Attention should here be called to the fact that the "*Hemingway Steamer*" is adapted for use for *heavy scraped corn* or corn cut and packed according to the Eastern process or "dry pack." It being understood that the grain being mixed with the scraping from the cob, it is readily worked through the machine, the machine not being adapted for *whole grain* corn or "*moist pack*."

The other method of handling heavy scraped or "dry packed" corn is as follows:

After leaving the "silking machine" the corn goes to the "*Warfield-Nichols Can Filler*," before described and shown on page 41. From the "Filler" the cans are wiped, go to the cappers (page 45), then to the "Exhauster" (page 46), and so on as before.

Without entering into the merits of the two principles of packing corn, viz. the "dry" or "moist" pack, it might be advisable to mention several facts in connection therewith, in order that the "uninitiated" may the better judge of the two "styles" or "systems." In the first place, it will be readily understood that when corn is cut and *scraped* (dry pack), the goods thereby produced will *pack closer* in the can than when cut *whole grain* ("moist" pack), thus requiring considerably more corn to *fill* a can than with "whole grain" corn. Also, the *process* is entirely different, very much longer time being required to cook the corn. In fact the two grades of corn are treated in an entirely different manner, the "dry" pack being of course the more expensive of the two. It might be well for the packer to pack some of each grade. And here comes in the value of the "Warfield Cutting Machine" (page 28), possessing as it does the advantage of adjustment for *either grade of goods*.

The packer of corn (and in fact *all canned goods*) should exercise particular care to have his corn run "regular" or "alike." To accomplish this result, he must sample the corn from time to time as it comes from the kettle, and whenever a "process" seems to be "off color," it should be set aside and not mixed with the good corn. Also have the "off" lots of corn on the ear kept separate from the good corn. It is essential to have the cans clean and bright, nicely labeled and put in clean boxes, carefully nailed. Neatness should be exercised from the cutting to the boxing of the goods.

TOMATOES.

The preparing of Tomatoes for the can has to be done largely by hand work, as up to this period no machine has been devised that will successfully remove the outer skin from the tomato, a most difficult problem indeed for the inventor to solve.

The most popular varieties for canning are the "New Queen," "Paragon," and "Acme."

The proper time to sow the seed is about April 10 to 15, the plants being set out about May 15th to May 25.

The setting out of tomato plants (and in fact all kinds of plants) was always done by hand previous to the introduction of the "McKay Patent Plant Setter," an extremely simple device by which any kind of plant can be set out in a far superior manner than can be accomplished by hand. This machine (a cut of which is shown on page 56) is manufactured exclusively by **The Warfield Manufacturing Company**, is cheap, effective, light and durable, and, apart from its superior setting of a plant, will do the work of some three or four hand "setters." The vines should be kept clean and well worked, and only *sound, ripe* tomatoes should be picked for the factory.

A fair *average* for a *crop* of tomatoes is about 200 to 250 bushels of good tomatoes per acre. As high as 600 bushels are grown to the acre, however. A bushel of *good, sound* tomatoes will fill when peeled from fourteen to sixteen 3-pound cans.

The factories usually open about August 20th and continue until the frost kills the vines. Tomatoes should be carried to the factory in bushel boxes. From the box they go to the "*Scalder.*" This apparatus consists of a perforated receptacle for the tomatoes, holding from two to three bushels. This receptacle is so hinged or pivoted over a tank adapted to hold water as to admit of its being lowered into the water and raised sufficiently high to allow the tomatoes when scalded to roll from the mouth of the receptacle into buckets. The "*Scalder,*" built by **The Warfield Manufacturing Company** (see cut on page 52) is a strong, simple device, carefully designed to prevent the bruising of the tomatoes during the " scalding " and emptying process.

Another method of scalding is to empty the tomatoes into wire baskets, which are dipped by hand into boiling water—a very slow process, however.

After being scalded they go to the "peelers" (about 3 cents per bucket being paid for peeling) and then are packed in the can.

· If it is desired to procure a machine for this purpose, in its selection care should be exercised to obtain one that will not *mash* and *tear* the tomatoes in the packing operation and thus deteriorate the quality of the goods. The cans should be filled with ripe, solid tomatoes, packed as "whole" as possible. (**The Warfield Manufacturing Company** will shortly put on the market a "Tomato Filler," which will combine large capacity with perfect work.)

After the cans are filled they are placed in trays, "wiped" and taken to the "*Warfield-Winters Capping Machine*" (page 45). It should be stated here that some packers do not "exhaust" tomatoes at all, but "tip" the cans after capping and put them in the process kettle ("Shriver" patent kettle, page 48, or "open" kettles, which require very much longer time to cook). The large majority of packers, however, prefer to "exhaust," contending that the goods are firmer and better, and the system a safer one. For the purpose of "exhausting" tomatoes or to cook same by *open bath process*, the "*Warfield-Winters Exhauster*" is the machine (page 46), giving every can the same heat, same time for exhaust or process (as case may be), and delivering the cans to the "*Warfield Test Tub*" (page 47). From the "test tub" they go to the kettle, then to "cooling tub" (if used), and then packed away.

If the *open-bath process* is used, the "*Warfield-Winters Exhauster*" is an admirable machine for processing the goods after the "exhaust," or, if packed without "exhaust," it can be used for this purpose equally well. It can be adjusted to give any time required by setting it to the proper speed.

PEAS.

The packing of Green Peas is a very particular operation, and the greatest care should be exercised in the various stages of their preparation for the can.

Peas for canning are divided into two classes—" Early June" and " Marrowfats."

In Maryland the factories open on " Early Junes" about June 1st, and continue on same until " Marrowfats" begin, about July 1st, ending about July 25th.

" Early Junes" are planted about the middle of April, and " Marrowfats" two weeks later.

There is perhaps no vegetable packed in which the yield per acre varies as much as in peas.

An acre of " Early Junes" will turn out, according to soil and season, from 20 to 60 bushels of peas in the pod, which will shell out from 14 to 16 cans.

An acre of " Marrowfats" will yield from 35 to 90 bushels, shelling out from 12 to 14 cans.

The peas are first hulled, and for this purpose the " *Swingle Patent Pea Huller*" should be employed. This machine is a very interesting piece of mechanism, cleaning the pods in a perfect manner, separating the shelled peas from the pods and delivering them to separate receptacles. It is built in two sizes, the largest size having a capacity of 1000 bushels per day, and the smaller size hulling 400 to 500 bushels per day. A cut of this machine is shown on page 53, **The Warfield Manufacturing Company** being sole manufacturers of the same. It is indispensable to packers of peas.

From the " *Huller*" the peas go to the " *Separator*" or " assorter," which " separates " or " grades " the peas into the various sizes.

This is probably the most important part of the preparation of the peas for the can—to have them properly " graded." For this purpose the " *Warfield Separator*" should be used.

This machine has a capacity of from 800 to 1000 bushels per day, and will grade the peas into four sizes. It has an adjustable self-feeding attachment (a difficult part of the operation, to *properly* feed the peas to the cylinder), and has many important features which long experience has suggested, not possessed by any other machine for this purpose manufactured.

Especial attention has been paid in the designing of the "*Separator*" to prevent " banking," " choking " or " clogging " of the peas, and easy cleaning of the machine.

As the *value* of your peas depends largely upon the proper *grading* of them, especial care should be used to procure the best machine for this purpose the market will afford. The cut on page 54 shows the " *Warfield Separator*." The Warfield Manufacturing Company, sole manufacturers of the same.

After the grading process, the peas, now kept separate according to size, are " blanched." This is accomplished by placing them in a perforated receptacle and immersing them in boiling water, preferably contained in a copper-jacket kettle.

After " blanching," they are filled into the cans (2 lb), then " dipped " in hot brine, or " hot dipped," as it is termed.

For this purpose the " *Warfield-Winters Dipping Machine* " should be employed (page 42). This machine performs the work perfectly, wire-gauze covers being used over the cans, and a coil of pipe placed in the machine to heat the brine. From the " Dipping Machine " the cans are placed in trays, wiped, and taken to the " *Warfield-Winters Capping Machine* " (page 45), capped, tipped, and then placed in the "*Shriver Process Kettle*" (page 48).

The young and tender peas are the most sought after by the buyer, such grades always being in good demand. Baltimore is the great " pea center " of the country, and gives employment to an immense army of workers in this branch of the canning industry.

STRING BEANS.

The preparing of String Beans for the can closely resembles the mode for handling peas.

After "stringing them" they are "blanched," put in 2-lb cans, "hot dipped" in " *Warfield-Winters Dipping Machine*," capped on capping machine, tipped, and put in process kettle.

LIMA BEANS.

The packing of Lima Beans is conducted in similar manner, excepting they are not "blanched."

They are shelled, put in 2-lb cans, "hot dipped" in " *Warfield-Winters Dipping Machine*," capped, tipped, and put in kettle; a bushel of shelled beans filling some 60 cans.

SUCCOTASH.

A very popular combination of sugar corn and lima beans, under the above term, is produced by setting the knives of the " *Warfield Cutting Machine* " to remove the grain as whole as possible from the cob, taking a *light scrape*, using about two-thirds corn to one-third lima beans, preparing for the kettle same as corn.

BERRIES.

Berries are placed in 2-lb cans, " hot dipped " in water or syrup, using the " *Warfield-Winters Dipping Machine*," capped, and put in process kettle. (See page 42.)

PEACHES.

"Always in season" are Peaches, properly put up. The factories of Maryland open on peaches in August and close last of September, giving employment, as in peas, to countless numbers of hands.

Baltimore is the center of the peach packing industry. Peaches are divided into "Extras," "Standards," "Seconds," and "Pie-fruit," and are pared principally by hand; the "extras," "standards" and "seconds" being pared and halved, "pie-fruit" being simply halved. They are packed in 2 and 3 lb cans—3 lb mostly. After being pared they are packed in the cans full, and "hot dipped" in either "hot syrup" or water, as the case may be, according to quality of goods desired.

For the purpose of "hot dip" the "*Warfield-Winters Dipping Machine*" is used, adapted for 3-lb cans, and provided with the coil of pipe as for peas, the machine being connected with the syrup or hot water cask, as for corn it is connected with the brine cask. This cask, preferably, contains a coil of pipe to assist in keeping the liquid therein hot.

From the "dipping machine" the cans are placed in trays, wiped, and taken to the capping machine (page 45), capped, tipped, and placed in process kettle (page 48).

One bushel of peaches will yield from 14 to 20 3-lb cans, according to quality of fruit and grade desired.

OYSTERS.

Now we come to "Maryland's pride," the oyster; and well may she feel proud, for the oysters of the Chesapeake Bay have achieved a world-wide reputation.

Baltimore is the center of the great oyster packing industry. Again are armies of workers employed in the various stages of the oyster trade.

The business growing out of the oyster product of the Chesapeake Bay employs about 1500 vessels and some 11,000 hands, while the employment of the various persons interested directly and indirectly supports some 150,000 people. The area of the oyster beds of the Chesapeake Bay and tributaries in 1884 was 123,520 acres, and the estimated ground capable of producing oysters was 640,000 acres.

The factories usually open for "steaming" oysters about October, closing about April.

The oysters in the shell are placed in cars holding about 12 bushels, which are run on tracks into the "steam box" holding two or three cars, where they are steamed.

The oyster car (page 55) manufactured by **The Warfield Manufacturing Company** for this purpose is strong, durable, and of the most approved pattern.

This Company also gives particular attention to the construction of "steam boxes" for this purpose.

After being steamed they are shucked, washed and put in the cans, then "hot dipped" in brine, capped, and put in process kettles. (See pages 42, 45, 48.)

Oysters are bought by measure regulated by law. The law also requires the weight of each can to be stamped on its cap. The laws of Maryland are very stringent regarding the packing of oysters. A bushel of oysters will shuck out from 35 to 60 ounces of meat.

As Baltimore is the Center of the Great Canning Industry of the Country,

So is she the home of the largest establishment for the manufacture of the *most complete line of canning-house machinery in the world*—The **Warfield Manufacturing Company.**

This Company, from its long and successful career in this line, possesses unsurpassed facilities for furnishing to the packer of canned goods *any article* of machinery he may require for the preparation of his fruits, vegetables, or oysters, for the can.

Its magnificent line of patented canning-house specialties —the very best in their particular department—is too well known to require further comment. They issue an illustrated catalogue, with cuts, full description, and testimonials of all their machinery, which is mailed, free of cost, to all applicants.

The Warfield Manufacturing Co.

MANUFACTURERS OF

Special Machinery,

BALTIMORE, MD.

DIRECTORS :

S. DAVIES WARFIELD,	. . . *President.*
CALVIN S. SHRIVER,	. . *Vice-President.*
C. TAYLOR JENKINS,	*Secretary and Treasurer.*

GEORGE CATOR,   ROBERT K. MARTIN,
R. EMORY WARFIELD,   GEORGE H. HOPE.

S. DAVIES WARFIELD, . . . *President and Gen'l Manager.*

SOLE MANUFACTURERS OF

Improved Corn Packing and Patented Canning House Machinery.

Fruit, Vegetable and Oyster Packers' Machinery,

STEAM ENGINES,

SHAFTING, HANGERS, PULLEYS, COUPLINGS & GENERAL MACHINE WORK.

Special Machinery Designed and Constructed.

STEAM AND WATER PIPE FITTING.

In order that the reader may form an intelligent idea
of the construction of the various appliances herein alluded
to for the preparation of Fruits and Vegetables for the
can, the following cuts are given, together with endorse-
ments from many well-known firms, which should be a
guarantee of the efficiency of the machinery described.

WARFIELD'S

LATEST

Improved Green Corn Cutter,

With Automatic Feed and Ear-Centering Attachment.

Positively the only Corn Cutting Machine manufactured that can be set so as to leave the grain *perfectly whole*, as in hand cutting, or can be set to cut and "scrape" at any depth desired.

Manufactured under Letters Patent of the United States, issued to S. D. WARFIELD, September 27, 1881; May 16, 1882; July 17, 1883; August 26, 1884; December 30, 1884; April 28, 1885. Other patents pending.

From the Proprietors of the Shriver Process Kettle.

THOS. J. MYER & Co., Baltimore, write:

"Your improved Corn Cutting Machine does its work well, and is one that will give entire satisfaction in every particular. We think no corn packer can do well without it in this progressive age."

———.

From the Patentee of the Fisher Process Kettle.

GEO. W. FISHER, Baltimore, writes:

"Your Cutter is unquestionably the best machine on the market for cutting green corn from the cob. It does its work perfectly, and I cheerfully recommend its use to all corn packers."

———

E. B. MALLORY & Co., Baltimore, Md., write:

"We shall want two more of your Corn Cutters for the coming season. Please book our order for same. We are very much pleased with the work your Cutters did this season; they proved satisfactory in every respect, and we would not think of packing corn without them. We have recommended all our customers who pack corn to use your machine, as the saving in cost of cutting the corn and the increased output to be obtained by using them will repay for the investment in a very short time."

———

GEORGE ACKERMANN, former superintendent A. Fischer & Co. (Star Preserve Works), Cincinnati, Ohio, writes:

"Your favor dated January 24 is received. In reply would say that Messrs. A. Fischer & Co. used your Corn Cutter last season while I superintended their factory at Lima, Ohio, and I can say that it worked to perfection. Having had the 'Sprague Cutter' in use at the same time, I found that the 'Warfield Cutter' did much cleaner and better work."

———

EVANS, DAY & Co., Indianapolis, Ind., write:

"We hand you check for $250. Please receipt bill and return. We intend giving you a testimonial, to be used as you see fit, setting forth the utility, completeness and effectiveness of your machine. It is worthy of the highest consideration, and fully demonstrates the practicability of cutting corn by machine in a most satisfactory manner."

WINTERS & PROPHET, Mt. Morris, N. Y., write:

" The two Corn Cutting Machines we bought of you this season have proven a grand success. Please enter our order for two more for next season. We have tried nearly every Corn Cutter offered on the market, and from our experience consider yours very much the best. In entering our order you will, of course, give us said machines at a price as low as you sell them during season of 1885."

A. COOLEY & BRO., Webster, Harford Co., Md., write:

"We used one of your Green Corn Cutters last season in our packing house, and were greatly pleased with it. We were prejudiced against all machines for cutting corn, as we had examined several cutters, but found none to do the work to our satisfaction. We are pleased to say that your machine far surpasses anything that we could expect, doing better work than can be done by hand, and at so much less cost. We averaged about 700 or 800 cans per hour. With good corn, we think there would be no trouble to cut 8000 or 10,000 cans in one day. We will put in another of your Cutters next year and do away with all hand cutting."

J. M. CUYKENDALL & CO., Hamilton, Ont., Canada, write:

" Your Corn Cutter works perfectly satisfactory, and we will need two more of them next season."

GADD & SUDLER, Sudlersville, Md., write:

" In reference to your Corn Cutter, we take pleasure in saying that we believe it to be the most durable and best adapted for all modes of cutting corn of any machine yet on the market."

J. S. WHITEFORD, Delta, Pa., writes:

" Yours received. Replying, would say your Corn Cutter gives entire satisfaction.

"You can fix the above as you like. I have used the '*Sprague*' and other Cutters, and compared to yours, I think they are a nuisance. My Cutter gave me better satisfaction than ever this year (being the third season). I cut with it and three girls, this year, 700 cases in one day. You may add any of this you want in my testimonial."

H. W. McCall, York, Pa., writes:
"Your Cutter is excellent and does good work."

J. L. Anderson & Sons, Mount Holly, N. J., write:
"The Warfield Corn Cutting Machine gave us excellent satisfaction this season."

S. B. Silver & Bro., Deer Creek, Md., write:
"The three Corn Cutters received from you we have run the past two seasons. They give entire satisfaction, and are the only Cutters we continue to use after giving several kinds a trial."

Preston, Evans & Co., Salem, Roanoke County, Va., write:
"In answer to your inquiry as to the power Cutter, we take pleasure in stating that it gives us entire satisfaction, doing all that is claimed for it. The use of the machine largely reduces the cost of packing corn, and also makes a much better article than corn cut by hand or by any other machine we have seen. We think no packer can afford to be without it."

J. B. Counselman & Co., Houston, Del., write:
"The Corn Cutter we purchased from you and used the past season gave us entire satisfaction. Having had considerable experience in corn cutting machinery, we unhesitatingly endorse it as being the best machine on the market of its kind."

Ranney, Doty & Phelps, Lewistown, Ill., write:
"Yours 4th inst. received and noted. In answer would say that we have used your Corn Cutter this season and have been highly

pleased with the work it has done. We have no hesitation in recommending it to any packer of sweet corn as a first-class machine in
every respect."

H. F. STERN, Zanesville, Ohio, writes:

"Regarding your recent inquiry regarding Corn Cutting Machine
purchased of you last season, will say that it works to my full satisfaction and I would not be without it; heretofore have cut all corn by
hand at a heavy expense, but will not do so again as long as I can
have it cut so cheaply and satisfactory by 'Warfield Green Corn
Cutter.'"

GEO. K. McGAW, Baltimore, Md., writes:

"It gives me pleasure to add my testimonial to the many you have
of the merit and satisfactory working of your Corn Cutting Machine.
The two I bought and used the past season did the work so well that
I herewith place my order with you for two more for next season."

VAN CAMP PACKING CO., Indianapolis, Ind., write:

"The Cutter works perfectly satisfactory and is fully up to your
guarantee."

JAMES T. WALKER, Perrymans, Harford Co., Md., writes:

"The two Cutters purchased from you were thoroughly satisfactory. Each machine will cut from 8000 to 9000 cans per day, and
apart from a decided improvement in the quality of machine-cut
corn over hand-cut, I found, after making several tests, that 50 lbs of
corn on the *ear* cut by the machine would yield from 5 to 6 lbs
more corn than when cut by hand, the machines being set to cut
close and taking a very light scrape. These are facts which, in my
judgment, should recommend your machine to every practical corn
packer in the trade."

C. A. RUTLEDGE & BRO., Taylor P. O., Harford County, Md., write:

"The two Cutters bought of you this season worked well and gave
perfect satisfaction, and we shall want two more of them next season.

For dispatch, efficiency and durability we believe it has no equal. . . .
We have given the green-corn cutter business a good deal of attention, having examined most Cutters that have been on the market,
and have seen none that we consider a practical machine except your
improved, which is a perfect success and the best machine, considering
all things, known. . . . We very cheerfully give this our testimonial as
to the merits of your machine."

A. FISCHER & Co., Star Preserve Works, Cincinnati, Ohio, write :

" In reply to your favor of 7th, would say we have used your Corn
Cutter at our Lima (Ohio) factory and found it *entirely satisfactory.*"

JAMES G. MCSPARRAN & Co., Greene P. O., Lancaster County, Pa.,
write :

" The Corn Cutter we bought from you, and used the season past,
gave the very best satisfaction.   It is far superior to any Cutter we
have seen, displacing, on a rough calculation, at least fifteen ordinary
hands, and perhaps more.   It never gets tired, nor strikes for higher
wages when corn comes in thickest.   It certainly gets more corn and
less cob—that is, more weight of good, honest corn from the cob—
than any hand cutter we have ever had ; *and we consider the corn
cut by your machine fully twenty-five per cent. better than that cut by
hand.*

" We extend to you our congratulations and thanks for the degree
of perfection reached in your machine, and shall want one and perhaps two more next year."

BENJ. SILVER, JR., Glenville, Harford Co., Md., writes :

" I have your favor asking my opinion in regard to your Corn
Cutters, and will say they worked perfectly, and I found they would
do just about what you claimed for them.   I must congratulate you
on that point, viz. claiming no more for your machine than it would
do.   Most inventors deal more sparingly with the truth.   My largest
day's run was 26,500 cans, cut between 6 A. M. and 7.30 P. M.   I
estimated that 19,000 of this number were cut by the two machines,
the balance being cut by hand.   You have a very good head on
you . . ."

PLATTE VALLEY CANNING CO., St. Joseph, Mo., write :

" We have used two of your Corn Cutting Machines the past season. They do better work than anything we have ever tried."

H. A. OSBORN, Havre de Grace, Md., writes :

" The Warfield Cutters I bought of you last season gave me entire satisfaction. They did their work perfectly, cut the grain just as I wanted it, and the corn is far superior to that cut by hand. Every corn packer should use your machine. My business will require one and perhaps two more of these Cutters the coming season."

McCONNELL, CLANCEY & CO., Chillicothe, Ohio, write :

" We have used your Corn Cutter for the past three (3) years and we find it gives general satisfaction in every particular. We have run it very steady each season, and except new knives and a few minor parts replaced, we have had no other repairs. We recommend it to all packers."

JOHNS H. JANNEY, Churchville, Harford Co., Md., writes :

"Yours was the only Corn Cutting Machine I ever felt inclined to try, and while I was convinced they would suit the Eastern or heavy pack, was doubtful whether they would prove a success when it was desired to cut the grain whole. The Cutters I bought of you will cut close to the cob with a very light scrape, thus suiting our Harford County style of packing. Your machine is a success, and every corn packer should have them."

HOPPER BROS., Havre de Grace, Md., write :

" We tried every kind of Corn Cutter known to us, but not until we tried yours did we experience satisfaction. Your machines are making a great improvement in the quality of the corn pack of this section. We hope you will turn your attention to other kinds of packing machinery with like success."

W. ELWOOD HARRY, Delta, Pa., writes :

" The Cutter is running beautifully. It gives perfect satisfaction, and only needs to be kept in order and fed plenty of green corn.

I have never run it slower than 60—generally 65. I am satisfied it will fill 9000 cans in 10 hours with the greatest ease in good corn."

R. EMORY & Co., Taylor P. O., Harford County, Md., write :

" The three Cutters purchased from you this season gave entire satisfaction in every particular. Having tested the ' Barker Cutter ' two years ago, and being compelled to lay them aside in consequence of their many imperfections, we were reluctant to take hold of any Cutter, knowing the extreme difficulty of producing a successful and practical corn-cutting machine.

" Yours is a *complete* success ; not only do you get a large increase in yield, but the corn is of so superior quality that no packer can *afford* to cut by hand. The difference in price on account of quality (which will be seen and appreciated by the consumer) will more than pay for the machine in one season, without regard to increase in yield and saving of labor. This is our opinion of your machine, and yours *only*, after having used or seen all machines now in use."

EDWARD H. HALL, Abington, Md., writes:

" While I must admit I was somewhat prejudiced against Corn Cutters before trying yours, after using the one bought from you the entire season, I will say it gave me the best satisfaction, and it cannot fail to supersede hand labor for cutting corn."

J. B. HANWAY, Joppa, Md., writes :

" Replying to your favor 8th, it is with great pleasure that I can cheerfully testify to the superior qualities of your improved ' Green Corn Cutter.' In all my interviews with you, you know how prejudiced I was against using Corn Cutters ; I now beg leave herewith to have you accept my sincere thanks and gratitude for your having recommended me so strongly to try one of yours. It was all that you claimed for it, and I will want one or two more next season."

GEO. F. WALKER, Bel Air, Md., writes :

" Having purchased of you, in July last, two of your Corn Cutters, I am free to say it is one of the most valuable canning-house implements of recent invention. They gave me entire satisfaction, cutting the corn much better than by hand. No canner can afford to be without one."

———

Geo. W. McComas, Clayton, Harford County, Md., writes:

" The Green Corn Cutter purchased of you in July gave me entire satisfaction. The quality of corn is improved over hand cut. It is a labor and money-saving machine. I wish you success in their introduction."

———

D. B. Chesney, Perrymans, Harford County, Md., writes:

" Nothing could have been more satisfactory to us than the Corn Cutting Machine we bought of you the past season. It did *more* than you claim for it."

———

A. Boyle, Delta, Pa., writes:

" I have used your Green Corn Cutter the last two years and it has done all you claim it to do."

———

A. H. Nelson & Bro., Perrymans, Md., write:

" The Corn Cutting Machine we purchased from you and used last season did its work well, and we are entirely satisfied with the same. We recommend it to every corn packer."

———

The Warfield Manufacturing Co., Baltimore, Md., are sole manufacturers of this Cutter, and in addition to the letters copied above, have numbers of others fully as strong, endorsing the machine as *unequaled* for its purpose. They issue an illustrated Catalogue, giving full description, price, etc., of this Cutter.

A SPECIAL

Gold Medal

*Was Awarded
this Machine by*

The Agricultural Society
of Baltimore Co., Md.

Timonium, October 2, 1884.

*Perfect in Operation. Durable in Construction. This Machine being Examined
by a Special Committee of Prominent Packers.*

Agricultural and Mechanical Society of Harford Co., Md.

REPORT OF SPECIAL COMMITTEE FOR 1884.

FAIR GROUNDS, BEL-AIR, MD., October 16th, 1884.

We, the undersigned, a Special Committee appointed to examine the
" WARFIELD GREEN CORN CUTTING MACHINE," after a full and careful examination of the same, at a trial made at the *Harford County Agricultural
Exhibition for* 1884, do hereby report :   That for durability, simplicity of construction, character of work performed and rapidity of motion, we believe that
it is the *best machine* offered to the Packers of corn *in the United States ;* and
we recommend that the patentee be awarded *a diploma* and the sum of *fifty
dollars* for the same.   It does its work beautifully.

(Signed), EDWARD H. HALL,
G. SMITH NORRIS,
W. H. SCHULL.

We, the undersigned, Packers of corn, having seen the practical working
of the machine, do hereby fully concur in the above. (Signed),

B. SILVER, JR.,
JAMES T. WALKER,
JOHNS H. JANNEY,
S. B. SILVER & BRO.,
S. N. HYDE & SON,
C. A. McGAW,

C. A. RUTLEDGE & BRO.,
B. EMORY & CO.,
JAMES F. KENLY,
GEO. W. ANDREWS,
W. R. & A. F. GALBREATH,
R. B. McCOY.

Agricultural and Mechanical Society of Harford Co., Md.

REPORT OF SPECIAL COMMITTEE FOR 1885.

FAIR GROUNDS, BEL-AIR, MD., October 17th, 1885.

The undersigned, the Committee on miscellaneous Exhibits, or having in
charge discretionary Premiums, having carefully examined the Machines exhi-
bited by The Warfield Manufacturing Company of Baltimore, for cutting the
grains of corn from the ear, for dipping the filled cans of corn in brine, and for
capping them ; and having, besides, personal knowledge of the excellence of
the work done by these machines in canning houses, earnestly recommend that
a premium of *one hundred dollars* be paid to the exhibitor of these machines,
as we believe them to be of the class to which the funds of the Society should
be paid—promoting as they do the success, in a material degree, of a great
industry. (Signed), GARRETT AMOS,
E. A. ALLEN,
WM. H. GRAY.

Warfield's Corn Silking Machine

(PATENT APPLIED FOR)

For Silking and Cleaning the Corn after it is Cut from the Cob.

AYLMER CANNING Co., Aylmer, Ont., write:

"We have used the Corn Silking Machine gotten from you in the spring, during the whole of the corn-packing season of 1887. It is strongly constructed and did its work to our entire satisfaction, and we have no hesitation in saying that it is the best Silker we have yet seen in operation."

E. B. MALLORY & Co., Baltimore, Md., write:

"We have used your new 'Corn Silking Machine' and have found it very satisfactory in every respect, especially on heavy scraped corn. We shall want two more the coming season."

JOHNS H. JANNEY, Churchville, Md., writes:

"Your Silker is the *best* machine for the business I have seen. I am well pleased with it."

THE TEKAMAH CANNING CO., Tekamah, Neb., write :

" Your Silker gives the best of satisfaction with us. Find it *simple*, durable, and having wonderful capacity. Always has been *in order* to do business since arrival. Shall depend on it to handle the product of from 40 to 60 tons corn per day for the coming season."

———

GEO. K. MCGAW, Baltimore, writes :

" It gives me pleasure to state that ' The Warfield Silking Machine ' used the past season did its work well and satisfactory."

———

J. W. CUYKENDALL & Co., Hamilton, Ont., Canada, write :

" Replying to your inquiry as respects the working of your ' Corn Silker ' which we purchased from you this year, would say, when it was delivered in our factory we were of the opinion it would not do the work, but are pleased to inform you we are well satisfied. It mixes the corn and silks it perfectly, and is so simple in construction that a small boy does all our work with it. We shall need at least one more Silker and Cutter the coming season, and will call and see you some time in January."

———

ONTARIO PRESERVING CO., Middleport, N. Y., write :

" Your favor received, and in reply would say that the Silker we bought of you and used the past season proved very satisfactory, and we are pleased to add our name to the many you have bearing evidences of its merits."

———

BENJ. SILVER, JR., Glenville, Harford County, Md., writes :

" Your Silker did very good work with two hands. We could run through it 30,000 cans in 10 hours, and if we had had the corn I believe it will silk 50,000 cans in 10 hours."

———

JAS. T. WALKER, Perrymans, Md., says :

" The Silker bought of you this season gave me entire satisfaction. It is the best machine I have ever seen for its purpose."

S. B. Silver & Bro., Deer Creek, Md., write :

" The Silker received from you in 1887 gives good satisfaction and is equal to any we have ever seen."

A. Cooley & Bro., Webster, Harford County, Md., write :

" We used one of your Silkers this year and were very much pleased with it. We think that no canner can pack corn without one. The machine will do the work better than can be done by hand."

James C. Jordan, Stewartstown, York County, Pa., writes :

" The Silking Machine that I bought from you the season just past did its work to my entire satisfaction."

Edward S. Edge, Darlington, Harford County, Md., writes :

" In reply to your favor 4th inst., I will say that your Silker is just the machine you represent it to be and that no canner should be without one. It does perfect work."

R. Emory, Taylor, Md., writes :

" I have used the Warfield Silker one year and found it did the work better than any I have used."

Wm. Hutchins, St. James P. O., Baltimore County, Md., writes :

" Your Corn Silking Machine should be in every packing house. I have used it and am well pleased with its work."

J. L. Richardson, Perrymans, Md., writes :

" I have used your Silker and consider it the best machine for the purpose manufactured."

D. G. McCoy, Rising Sun, Cecil County, Md., writes :

" The new and improved Silker you sold me this season worked excellent. Every particle of filth is taken out and the corn left beautifully clean."

The Warfield-Nichols Can Filler.

(PATENT PENDING)
For Automatically Filling Cans with Corn, &c.
Every Can Filled Alike.

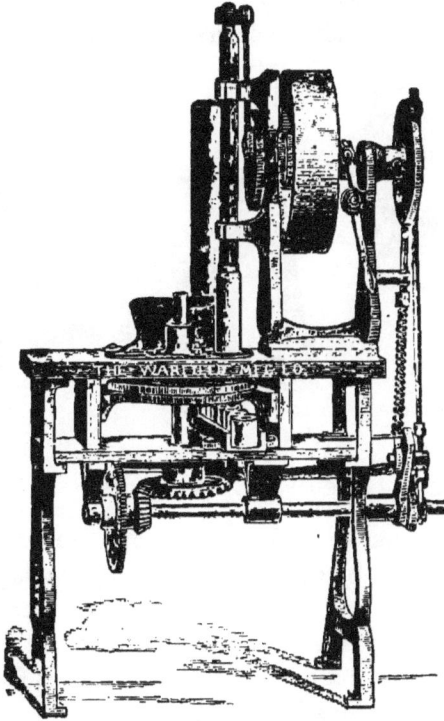

This machine automatically carries the cans to the filling mechanism, where the desired amount of corn is filled into the can, then discharges the filled can from the machine at other end. It can be adjusted to put any desired quantity into the can.

Refer to
> MR. J. M. HAYNER, South Lebanon, Ohio.
> MESSRS. C. E. SEARS & CO., Circleville, Ohio.
> MESSRS. SEARS & NICHOLS, Chillicothe, Ohio.

Manufactured exclusively by The Warfield Manufacturing Co. Full description, etc., in their Illustrated Catalogue.

Warfield-Winters Can Dipping Machine

(PATENTED MARCH 14, 1882)

For Automatically Filling Cans or Jars with Brine, Syrup, or other
Liquids, and Draining Same.

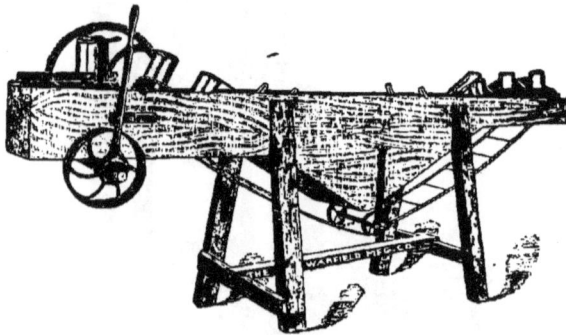

McSparran & Co., Green P. O., Pa., write:

"We cannot speak too highly in commendation of your Can
Dipping Machine used by us last season. It is a superlative success,
it is perfect. What more need we say? It is economical, system-
atizing and cleanly. We consider the fact that all cans coming from
it equally full of brine is alone yearly worth to us four times the cost
of the machine, in improved market value of our corn. We will be
pleased to have you refer to us if in need of any good words for
your Dipper.

"N. B.—We will likely want from one to three more Cutters next
season."

H. A. Osborn, Havre de Grace, Md., writes:

"Your Can Dipping Machine for brining corn is a great success.
Every can is filled and drained alike, and it certainly is much cleaner
than the old way of filling by hand. It will entirely supersede hand
dipping, beyond a doubt."

PRESTON, EVANS & CO., Salem, Roanoke County, Va., write :

" The Warfield-Winters Dipping Machine is a success, and we regard it as an indispensable piece of packing-house machinery."

JOHNS H. JANNEY, Churchville, Harford County, Md., writes:

" In reply to your inquiry as to how I like your Dipper, I take pleasure in saying that it is a complete success, and the only machine I ever encountered that does *more* than it was represented to do and does it *well.* I like to watch it at work."

HOPPER BROS., Havre de Grace, Md., write :

" We have used your Dipping Machine in packing our corn for the past two seasons, and have never seen any machine better adapted to its purpose. We can readily run 25,000 cans per day through it. It requires but little attention, and a child can operate it."

JAMES C. JORDAN, Stewartstown, York County, Pa., writes :

" I used your Can Dipping Machine during the past season and think every packer should have them."

JAMES T. WALKER, Perrymans, Harford County, Md., writes:

" Your Dipping Machine for filling corn cans with brine is simply *perfect.* No corn-packer after seeing it in operation would ever be without it."

A. BOYLE, Delta, Pa., writes :

" Your Dipping Machine since your late improvement has given entire satisfaction."

J. B. HANWAY, Joppa, Md., writes:

" I take great pleasure in adding my testimony to the many you have of the superior quality of your Can Dipping Machine; it is just perfect, dipping and draining every can alike, and much cleaner and quicker than dipping by hand. I consider it one of the best and most important machines used in the packing business."

___

EDW. S. EDGE, Darlington, Harford County, Md., writes:

"In reply to your inquiry in regard to your Dipping Machine, will say that I have used it during the past season and find it will do all you claim for it. It is perfect in its operation, and does away with all possibility of light cans, besides doing the work at much less cost than the old manner of hand dipping. One machine is capable of dipping 20,000 cans per day of ten hours."

___

JAMES L. RICHARDSON, Perrymans, Md., writes:

"Your Dipping Machine for filling cans with brine is far superior to the old hand method of dipping, and is one of the most complete machines in the packing business."

___

S. B. SILVER & BRO., Deer Creek, Harford County, Md., write:

"We have used your Dipping Machine two seasons. We are very much pleased with it and would not be without it."

___

C. P. MITCHELL & BRO., Perrymans, Md., write:

"The Dipping Machine we bought from you two years ago gives entire satisfaction, and would not be without it for double the price of it."

___

D. B. CHESNEY, Perrymans, Md., writes:

"Your Dipping Machine gave us the best satisfaction."

___

BENJ. SILVER, JR., Glenville, Harford County, Md., writes:

"Your Dipping Machine is surely more cleanly and far preferable than the old hand way of dipping cans."

___

The Warfield Manufacturing Co., sole manufacturers of this machine. Price, etc., in their Illustrated Catalogue.

45

The Warfield-Winters Capping Machine.

(PATENTED APRIL 4, 1882)

For Capping Any Sized Can.

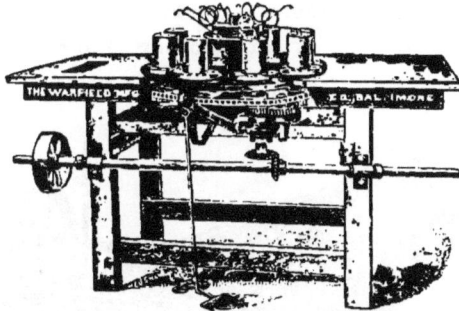

JAS. T. WALKER, Perrymans, Harford Co., Md., writes:
"The three Capping Machines I bought from you this season gave me entire satisfaction. I think your Capper will save about as much labor as any machine you manufacture, and would not be without them."

D. G. McCOY, Rising Sun, Cecil Co., Md., writes:
"The Capping Machine I bought of you saved enough in solder to pay my hand capper every day. I shall want another next season."

H. A. OSBORN, Havre de Grace, Md., writes:
"I did all my capping on the Capping Machines purchased from you last season, and found them entirely satisfactory. They make a firmer cap than by hand and at much less cost. It is the best machine I have ever seen for the purpose. Shall probably require another next season."

Messrs. Hollis, Matthews & Co., Perrymans, Md.; Messrs. R. Emory & Co., Taylor P. O., Md.; Messrs. Winters & Prophet, Mt. Morris, N. Y., and many others.

Manufactured solely by The Warfield Manufacturing Co., Baltimore. Full description and price in their Illustrated Catalogue.

The Warfield-Winters Exhauster.

(PATENTED MARCH 14, 1882)

For Exhausting Goods Previous to their Entrance to the Process
Kettle, or for Cooking Same.

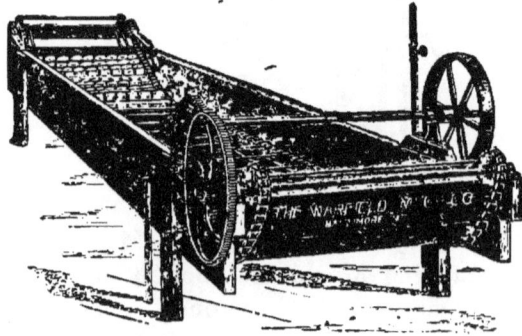

HOPPER BROS., Havre de Grace, Md., write:

"We consider your Exhausting Apparatus a great success.
There is no doubt but that it has saved us hundreds of dollars in
the last two seasons.

"It requires no taking of time, no skilled attention. *It makes
no mistakes.* It is safe and economical, and should be in every
factory."

Also, Messrs. C. E. Sears & Co., Circleville, Ohio; Messrs.
Winters & Prophet, Mt. Morris, N. Y.; Messrs. Hollis, Matthews &
Co., Perrymans, Md., and others.

The Warfield Manufacturing Co., Baltimore, sole manufacturers. Full description and price will be found in their
Illustrated Catalogue.

The Warfield Test Tub.

(PATENT PENDING)

For Testing Cans after Capping and Tipping.

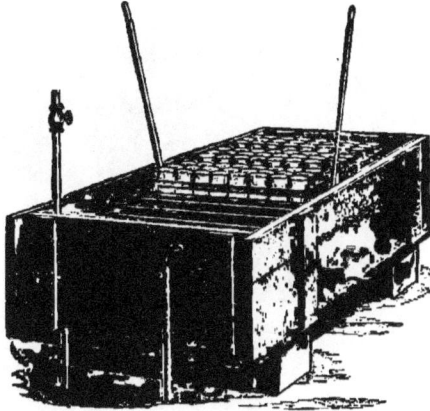

This machine is of simple construction and shows for itself. It is universally endorsed as the best style of " test apparatus " known.

The Warfield Manufacturing Co., Baltimore, are sole manufacturers. Illustrated Catalogue contains full description and price.

The Shriver Process Kettle.

The only Kettle whose Patents cover the right to use either the Dry Steam or Steam and Water Process.

There are seven or eight hundred of these Kettles in use. Copies of letters are unnecessary. It is known to every packer of canned goods, and the "Shriver Process Patents" acknowledged to be the best in use. This kettle is built in two sizes.

The Warfield Manufacturing Co., Baltimore, are sole manufacturers of this Kettle. Full description, prices, etc., to be found in their Illustrated Catalogue.

The Hemingway Corn Steamer.

(PATENTED APRIL 30, 1878.)

For Steaming Corn before going into Process Kettle.

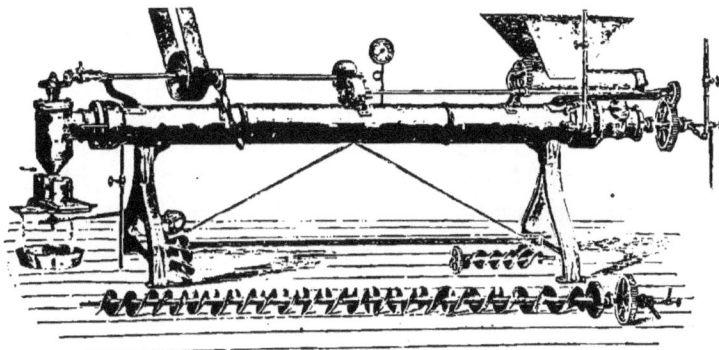

This machine is built in two sizes.

FORRESTVILLE CANNING CO., Forrestville, N. Y., write :

"Your favor of the 10th at hand, and regarding the Corn Cooker purchased of you and used by us this present season, would say it has done excellent work, and given perfect satisfaction in every respect."

FRANKLINVILLE CANNING CO., Franklinville, N. Y., write :

"We have used two of your Corn Cookers this season and are highly pleased with them. They work perfectly and produce the finest quality of goods. We have not had five swelled cans in 200,000, except occasionally a leaker."

DELHI FRUIT & VEGETABLE CANNING CO., Delhi, Ont., write:

"In reply to yours of the 23d, the Corn Cooker purchased of you last August has given perfect satisfaction. We cooked and filled over 300,000 cans with it, running on an average over 1000 cans per hour. Have run as many as forty-seven cans per minute."

ELGIN (IOWA) CANNING CO., Elgin, Iowa, write :

" We desire to say that the Cooker bought from you did its work to our entire satisfaction. It did much more work than you recommended. You claimed for it a capacity of 1000 cans per hour ; it did 1800 per hour for us and gave us no trouble, and we have had no trouble from swells."

BLOSSVALE CANNING CO., Blossvale, write :

" We have used one of your Corn Cookers the past season, with self-feeder attached. Have put through 250,000 cans with it, and it has given entire satisfaction. Have put through at the rate of 1200 cans per hour, and find that it cooks the corn very evenly."

SMITH, YINGLING & Co., Westminster, Md., write :

" We used, during the past season, one of your large size Cookers, and are glad to bear testimony of its efficiency. It took us a little time to get used to it, and especially to adjusting the filler table, of which you say you have now an improved pattern.

" We consider the quality of corn produced by it superior to any we have before packed, and it is a source of gratification that our buyers bear this same testimony. We can, without any trouble, pack 2000 cans an hour with it. Don't see how we could have done without it this past season.

" Wishing you deserved success, we remain."

THE WEBSTER PRESERVING CO., Webster, N. Y., write:

" We take pleasure in recommending the Hemingway Corn Cooker to any who may wish to avail themselves of a first-class cooker.

" We have used one of his machines in our factory the past two seasons, and the popularity of our corn is in a great measure due to the use of the Hemingway Cooker. It has been entirely satisfactory to us, and we regard it as the best Cooker with which we are acquainted, and the only correct process of putting up corn."

McGANNON & FAY PACKING CO., Carthage, Mo., write:

" In reply to your favor of the 1st inst., the Corn Cooker that we purchased of you this season gave excellent satisfaction. We prefer it to any we have seen. The corn goes through the machine in shorter space of time, leaving it much brighter in the cans."

———

J. B. McNABB, Salem, Ohio, writes:

"Yours at hand and carefully noted. In answer would say it is not often I put my name to a testimonial, and when I do there must be merit in the article in question. As to your Cooker, in its construction I have found it strong and durable. As to the quality of goods it produces, my customers say the quality is most excellent. As to the capacity of your Cooker, we have cooked and filled at the rate of twenty-eight cans per minute, and do not know how much more it could do if pushed. This we did with ease, one boy handling the cans at the machine. Have had no swelled cans, and your Cooker does very even work, does not choke or blow out, and is as much ahead of Merrill & Soule's Cooker as the Pullman car is ahead of the old lumbering stage-coach of years ago. You are to be congratulated on the success you have attained. Mr. Walter Phelps, my foreman (formerly of Camden, N. J.), co-operates with me in complimenting you on the success of your Cooker."

The Warfield Tomato Scalder.

For Scalding Tomatoes before Peeling.

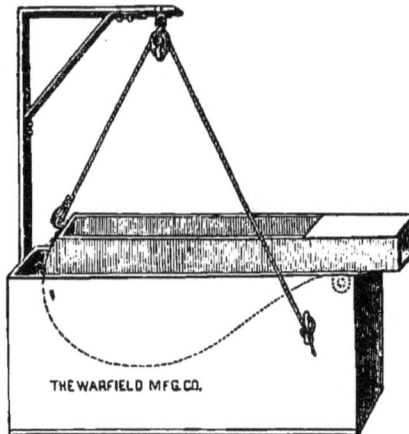

An admirable machine for the purpose and universally liked. In its construction especial care has been used to prevent "mashing" of the tomatoes.

Manufactured by The Warfield Manufacturing Co., Baltimore, and fully described in their Illustrated Catalogue.

The Swingle Pea Huller.

(PATENTED NOV. 20, 1883, MARCH 18, 1884.)

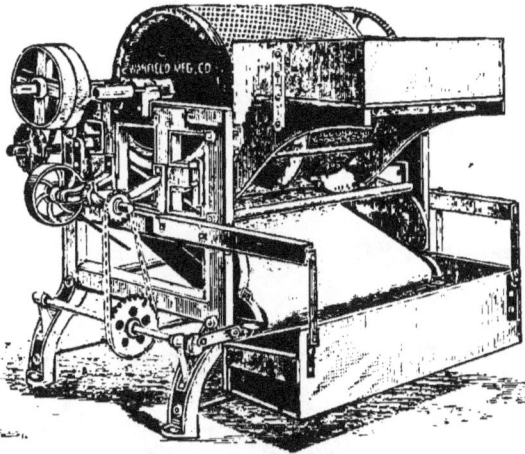

Messrs. E. B. MALLORY & Co., Baltimore, Md., write:

"The four Swingle Pea Hullers we purchased from you and used during the packing season did excellent work. We believe this machine is founded on the true principle for shelling peas, and when you enlarge its capacity, as you propose and can very readily do, it will be one of the most valuable machines for packers' use we know of."

Messrs. GREENABAUM BROS., Seaford, Del., write:

"We take pleasure in stating that we hulled all our peas on the two Swingle Pea Hullers purchased from you last spring, and that they performed their work very satisfactorily."

This machine is built in two sizes by the sole manufacturers, The Warfield Manufacturing Co., Baltimore. Their Illustrated Catalogue contains full description, etc.

The Warfield Pea Separator.

For Separating or "Grading" the Peas into different sizes.

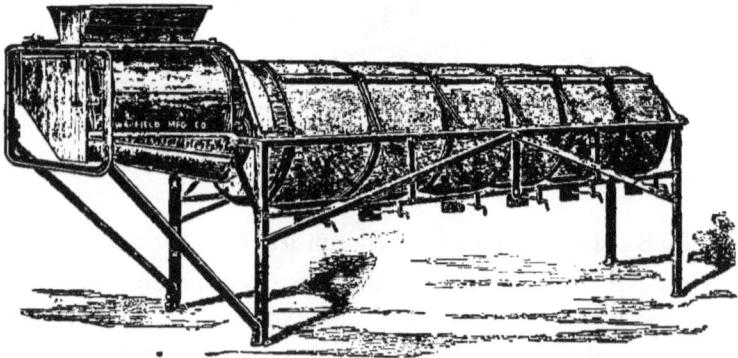

This machine is carefully designed and constructed, and has large capacity. It is conceded to be the best machine for its purpose on the market.

The Warfield Manufacturing Co., sole manufacturers. Their Illustrated Catalogue contains full description and price.

The Warfield Manufacturing Co.

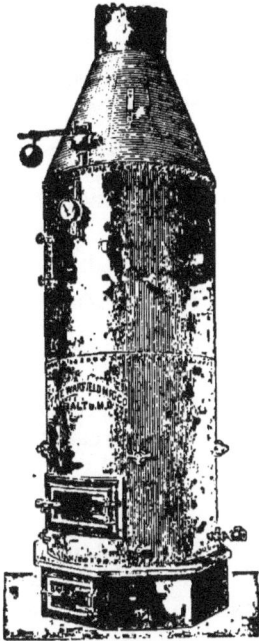

Crates, all sizes, of most approved patterns.

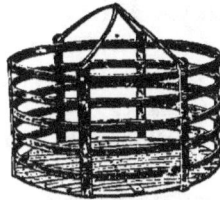

Floor Truck.

Boilers, all sizes, vertical and horizontal.

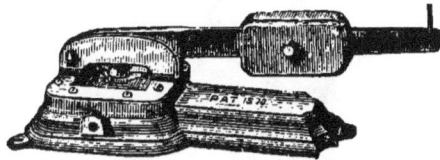

Damper Regulator. For regulating the draft on steam boilers. Saving of fuel will pay for this machine in a short time.

Crane Fixtures. Especially designed for Packers' use.

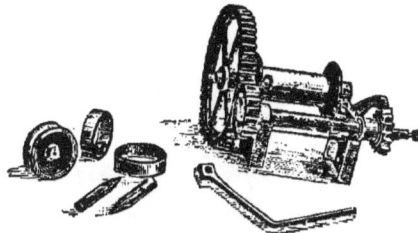

Steam Engines. All sizes, vertical and horizontal.

Oyster Car. All sizes, of most approved design.

Also, Open Process Kettles, Gasoline Tanks and Pumps, Fire Pots, Oyster Measures, Steam Box Doors and Fixtures, Steam Pumps, Injectors, Ejectors, Steam Gauges, Thermometers, Capping Irons, Forging Stakes, Furnace Doors and Grate Bars, Platform Scales, Coppers, etc.

The McKay Plant Setter.

(PATENTED JAN. 30, 1877, OCT. 2, 1888.)

The only Machine manufactured that will successfully set Plants of any Description—Tobacco Plants, Tomato Plants, Cabbage Plants, Sweet Potato Plants, Strawberry Plants.

Any kind or species of plant can be set in a far superior manner than can be done by hand.

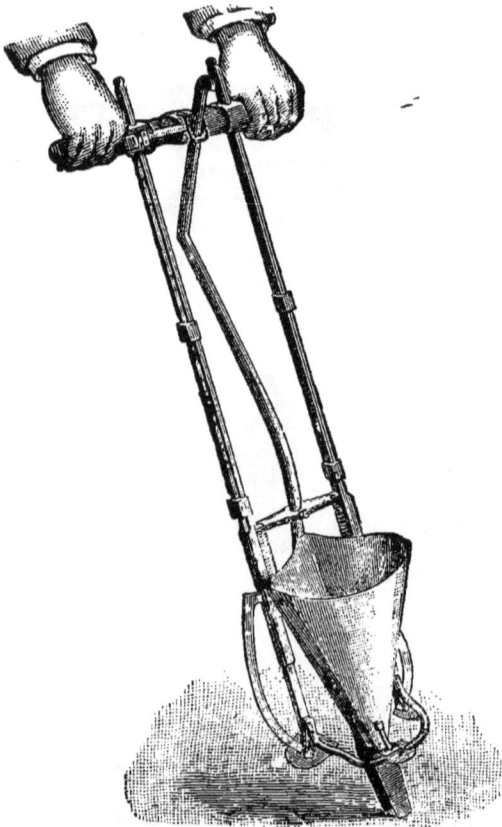

Over 200 sold by *one Agent*, in *one County*, in *one month*.

To all the weary workers who yearly wear themselves out setting plants, stooping over their work, rest is at hand.

Plants are set quicker, plants are set better, plants are set straighter, plants are covered nicer, plants will grow faster, than when set by hand.

It saves time, it saves labor, it saves stooping, it works well in *dry* ground, it works well in *wet* ground.

It opens the ground, does not *plaster* the sides of the hole as when setting with the "peg" or by hand; puts the plant in the ground and presses the earth around the *roots*, not at the *bud*, all at *one stroke*, without *stooping*.

It is simple, light, effective and cheap.

Truckers need it, gardeners require it, nurserymen want it, tomato growers must have it, and tobacco planters cannot do without it ; in fact, it is an indispensable article on the farm. **PRICE $7.00.**

The Warfield Manufacturing Co., sole manufacturers, 336, 338, 340 and 342 North Street, Baltimore, Md. Manufacturers of Special Machinery, Fruit and Vegetable Packers' Machinery of every description. Agents wanted in every County in the United States. Will lease State and County rights to the proper parties.

Useful Information.

Apples.—Pared and cored, clear in color, cans to be full of fruit, put up in water.

Blackberries.—Cans to cut out not less than two-thirds full after draining ; fruit to be sound, put up in water.

Cherries.—White Wax. Cans to be full of fruit, free of specks and decay, put up in not less than ten degrees of cold cane sugar syrup.

Cherries.—Red. Cans full of fruit, free of specks or decay, put up in water.

Gooseberries.—Cans to cut out not less than two-thirds full after draining, fruit unripe and uncapped, put up in water.

Egg Plums and Green Gages.—Cans full, whole fruit, free from reddish color or specks, put up in not less than ten degrees of cold cane sugar syrup.

Peaches.—Cans full, fruit good size, evenly pared, cut in half pieces, put up in not less than ten degrees of cold cane sugar syrup.

Pie Peaches.—Cans full, fruit sound, unpared, cut in half pieces, put up in water.

Pears.—Bartlett. Cans full, fruit white and clear, pared, cut in half or quarter pieces, put up in not less than ten degrees of cold cane sugar syrup.

Pears.—Bell or Duchess. Cans full, fruit pared, cut in half or quarter pieces, put up in not less than ten degrees of cold cane sugar syrup.

Pine Apples.—Cans full, fruit sound and carefully pared, slices laid in evenly, put up in not less than ten degrees of cold cane sugar syrup.

Plums and Damsons.—Cans full, sound fruit, put up in water.

Quinces.—Cans full, fruit pared and cored, cut in half or quarter pieces, put up in not less than ten degrees of cold cane sugar syrup.

Raspberries.—Cans to cut out not less than two-thirds full after draining, fruit to be sound, put up in not less than ten degrees of cold cane sugar syrup.

Strawberries.—Cans to cut out after draining not less than half full of fruit, which shall be sound and not of the varieties known as seedlings, put up in not less than ten degrees of cold cane sugar syrup.

Whortleberries.—Cans full, fruit to be sound, put up in water.

VEGETABLES.

Lima Beans.—Cans full of green beans, clear liquor.

String Beans.—Cans full, beans young and tender and carefully strung, packed during growing season.

Corn.—Sweet corn only to be used, cut from the cob while young and tender, cans to cut out full of corn.

Peas.—Cans full of young and tender peas, free of yellow or black eyes, liquor clear.

Pumpkin.—To be solid packed as possible, free from lumps and of good color.

CANNED GOODS LAW OF MARYLAND.

APPROVED BY THE GOVERNOR, APRIL 7, 1886.

SECTION 1. *Be it enacted by the General Assembly of Maryland*, That it shall be unlawful in this State for any packer of or dealer in hermetically canned or preserved fruits, vegetables or articles of food (excepting oysters), to sell such canned or preserved fruits, vegetables or other articles of food aforesaid, unless the cans, jars or vessels which contain the same shall bear the name and address of the person, firm or corporation that canned or packed the article, or the name of the dealer who purchases the same from the packer or his agent; such name and address shall be plainly printed on the label in letters not less than three-sixteenths of an inch in height and one-eighth of an inch in breadth, together with a brand-mark or term indicating clearly the grade or quality of the article contained therein.

SEC. 2. *And be it enacted*, That all packers and dealers in " Soaked Goods," put up from products dried or cured before canning or sealing, shall in addition to complying with the provisions of section one of this Act, cause to be printed plainly diagonally across the face of the label in good legible type, one-half of an inch in height and three-eighths of an inch in width, the words " Soaked Goods."

SEC. 3. *And be it enacted*, Any person, firm or corporation violating any of the provisions of this Act shall be deemed guilty of a misdemeanor and fined not less than fifty dollars nor more than one thousand dollars, to be recovered by indictment in any court in this State having criminal jurisdiction, one-half of said fine to be paid to the informer and the other half to the State Treasury, as other fines are paid.

SEC. 4. This Act shall take effect from November 1, 1886.

NEW YORK CANNED GOODS BILL.

CHAPTER 269. An act in relation to canned or preserved food; passed May 12, 1885; three-fifths being present. The people of the State of New York, represented in Senate and Assembly, do enact as follows:

SECTION 1. It shall hereafter be unlawful in this State for any packer of or dealer in hermetically sealed, canned or preserved fruits, vegetables or other articles of food, to sell or. offer such canned or preserved articles for sale, for consumption in this State, after January 1, eighteen hundred and eighty-six, unless the cans or jars which contain the same shall bear the name, address and place of business of the person, firm or corporation that canned or packed the article so offered, or the name of the wholesale dealer in this State who sells or offers the same for sale; together in all cases with the name of the State, county and city, town or village, where the same were packed, plainly printed thereon, preceded by the words " Packed at." Such name, address and place of business shall be plainly printed on the label, together with a mark or term indicating clearly the grade or quality of the article contained therein.

SEC. 2. All packers of and dealers in soaked goods or goods put up from products dried or cured before canning, shall in addition to complying with the provisions of section one of this act, cause to be plainly branded on the face of the label in good legible type, one-half of an inch in height and three-eighths of an inch in width, the word " Soaked."

SEC. 3. All goods packed prior to the passage of this act, and all goods imported or to be imported from foreign countries of foreign manufacture, are exempted from the provisions of this act.

SEC. 4. Any packer or dealer who shall violate any of the provisions of this act shall be deemed guilty of a misdemeanor, and punished by a fine of not more than fifty dollars for each offense in the case of retail dealers, and in the case of wholesale dealers and packers by a fine of not less than five hundred dollars nor more than one thousand dollars for each offense. The terms "packer" and "dealer" as used in this act shall be deemed to include any firm or corporation doing business as a dealer in or packer of the articles mentioned in this act. It shall be the duty of any board of health in this State cognizant of any violation of this act to prosecute any person, firm or corporation which it has any reason to believe has violated any of the provisions of this act, and the court or officer receiving the fine under any conviction under this act, after deducting the cost of trial and conviction, shall pay the same over to the board of health prosecuting the case. In case such offense is not prosecuted by any board of health, the fine received shall be disposed of in the manner now provided for.

STANDARD SIZES FOR CANS,

Adopted by the Baltimore Canned Goods Exchange, November 19, 1883.

	Diameter.	Height.
No. 1 Cans	$2\frac{3}{4}$ in.	4 in.
No. 2 Cans	3 7-16 in.	4 9-16 in.
No. 3 Cans	4 3-16 in.	$4\frac{7}{8}$ in.
No. 6 Cans, twice the quantity of No. 3.		
No. 10 Cans	$6\frac{1}{4}$ in.	7 in.

STANDARD SIZES OF BOXES.

Sizes of Boxes for Canned Goods—inside measurement.

2 dozen Cans, size 1	$11\frac{1}{2}$x $8\frac{1}{2}$x $8\frac{1}{4}$	inches.
2 " " " 2	$14\frac{1}{4}$x$10\frac{1}{2}$x $9\frac{1}{2}$	"
2 " " " 3	$17\frac{1}{4}$x13 x$10\frac{1}{4}$	"
4 " " " 1	$16\frac{1}{2}$x$11\frac{1}{4}$x $8\frac{1}{4}$	"
1 " " " 1, flat	$11\frac{1}{2}$x $8\frac{1}{2}$x $4\frac{1}{4}$	"
1 " " " 2, flat	$14\frac{1}{4}$x$10\frac{1}{2}$x $4\frac{3}{4}$	"
$\frac{1}{2}$ " Gallon Cans	19 x$12\frac{3}{4}$x $7\frac{1}{4}$	"
1 " " " high boxes	19 x$12\frac{3}{4}$x14	"
1 " " " flat boxes	$25\frac{1}{4}$x19 x 7	"
1 " No. 6 Cans	$20\frac{5}{8}$x$15\frac{3}{8}$x $6\frac{7}{8}$	"

SIZES OF TIN PLATE USED IN CANMAKING.

I. C. 14x20, Coke	B. V. Grade.
I. C. 12x12, Coke	B. V. Grade.
I. C. 13x26, Coke	B. V. Grade.
I. C. 14x20	I. B. Grade.
I. C. 14x20	Charcoal.

SHIPPING WEIGHTS FOR CANNED GOODS.

No. 1 Boxes	26 pounds.
No. 2 Boxes	46 pounds.
No. 3 Boxes	70 pounds.

STEAM.

A cubic inch of water evaporated under ordinary atmospheric pressure is converted into a cubic foot of steam (approximately).

Steam at atmospheric pressure flows into a vacuum at the rate of about 1550 feet per second, and into the atmosphere at the rate of 650 feet per second.

27.222 cubic feet of steam weigh 1 lb; 13.817 cubic feet of air weigh 1 lb.

The best designed boilers, well set, with good draft and skillful firing, will evaporate from 7 to 10 lbs of water per lb of first-class coal. The average result is from 25 to 60 per cent below this.

In calculating horse-power of tubular or flue boilers, consider 15 square feet of heating surface equivalent to one nominal horse-power.

One square foot of grate will consume on an average 12 lbs of coal per hour.

Locomotives average a consumption of 3000 gallons of water per 100 miles run.

WEIGHT AND COMPARATIVE FUEL VALUE OF WOOD.

One cord air-dried hickory or hard maple weighs about 4500 lbs, and is equal to about 2000 lbs coal.

One cord air-dried white oak weighs about 3850 lbs, and is equal to about 1715 lbs coal.

One cord air-dried beech, red oak or black oak weighs about 3250 lbs, and is equal to about 1450 lbs coal.

One cord air-dried poplar, chestnut or elm weighs about 2350 lbs, and is equal to about 1050 lbs coal.

One cord air-dried average pine weighs about 2000 lbs, and is equal to about 925 lbs coal.

From the above it is safe to assume that 2¼ lbs of dry wood is equal to 1 lb average quality of soft coal, and that the fuel value of the same *weight* of different woods is very nearly the same—that is, a pound of hickory is worth no more for fuel than a pound of pine,

assuming both to be dry.   It is important that the wood be dry, as
each 10 per cent of water or moisture in wood will detract about 12
per cent from its value as fuel.

WATER.—About 30 feet is the practical limit to which water can
be raised by suction.   Doubling the diameter of a pipe increases its
capacity four times.   Friction of liquids in pipes increases as the
square of the velocity.

RULES FOR CALCULATING THE SPEED OF PULLEYS AND GEARS.

In calculating for gears, multiply or divide by the number of teeth
as may be required.   In calculating for pulleys, multiply or divide
by their diameter in inches.

The driving wheel is called the *Driver*, and the driven wheel the
Driven.

TO FIND THE DIAMETER OF THE DRIVING PULLEY.

Multiply the diameter of the driven pulley, in inches, by its
required number of revolutions, and divide this product by the
number of revolutions of the driver.   The quotient will be the
diameter of the driving pulley in inches.

TO FIND THE DIAMETER OF THE DRIVEN PULLEY.

Reverse the above operation, multiplying together diameter of
driving pulley and its number of revolutions, and dividing product
by required number of revolutions of driven.   The quotient will be
the diameter of the driven pulley.

TO FIND THE NUMBER OF REVOLUTIONS OF THE DRIVEN PULLEY.

Multiply the diameter of the driver by its number of revolutions,
and divide the product by the diameter of the driven pulley.   The
quotient will be the number of revolutions of the driven pulley.

www.ingramcontent.com/pod-product-compliance
Lightning Source LLC
Chambersburg PA
CBHW021524090426
42739CB00007B/772